Anna Stenmark

Being in the Now coloring book

50 mindfulness quotes

Welcome to the calming world of coloring!

This book contains mindfulness quotes and illustrations.
They will take you on a journey to inner calm.

Feel free to use colored pencils,
pens, markers or gel pens to color the pictures.
Coloring pencils are the most versatile
as they allow you to add shading
and blend different colors together.
However, if you prefer to use markers or gel pens,
place a blank sheet under the page
to protect the picture beneath.

Once you have finished your artwork, cut out the page
and display it as an ongoing inspiration.

Enjoy your moments of coloring and being in the now!

CreateSpace, Washington DC

Designer © Anna Stenmark 2015, 2016
Drawings © cover and pp. 3, 39 irinarivoruchko; pp. 5, 45, 49 alexcoolok; pp. 7, 9, 33, 37, 59, 69 gollli; p. 11 Alina Shestialtinova; pp. 13, 47, 79 Alisa Foytik; pp. 15, 71, Yevheniia Hulinska; pp. 17 oksanaok; p. 19 Andrey KOTKO; p. 21 nataleana; p. 23 Alena Silkova; p. 25 Roman Dekan; p. 27 Alexey Bannykh; p. 29, 95 Volha Kavalenkava; p. 31 Yulia Snegireva; p. 35 alexokokok; p. 41 bryljaev; p. 43 Amicabel; pp. 51, 53, 57, 83 Chi Chiu Tse; pp. 55, 61, 77 Olesya Karakotsya; p. 63 matorinni; p. 65 Ghenadie Pascari; pp. 67, 75 Regina Jersova; p. 73 Jitka Martinkovičová; p. 81 Simonas Sileika; p. 85 red33; pp. 87, 101 pakete; p. 89 Marina Troshenkova; p. 91 Ionut Dan Popescu; p. 93 Natalya Belinskaya; p. 99 magenta10; p. 97 suriko8 | 123rf.com

First published in Great Britain 2015 by Luscious Books Ltd

The quotations in this book have been attributed where known.

ISBN 978-1523472857

A quiet mind
is all
you need.

All else

will happen rightly,

once your mind is quiet.

Sri Nisargadatta Maharaj

HAPPINESS IS . . .

WHEN YOU STOP WAITING

AND START MAKING
THE MOST OF THE MOMENT
YOU ARE IN NOW

DON'T LET YESTERDAY USE UP TOO MUCH OF TODAY.

CHEROKEE PROVERB

Starting today,
forget what's gone,
appreciate what's here
and look forward to
what's coming next.

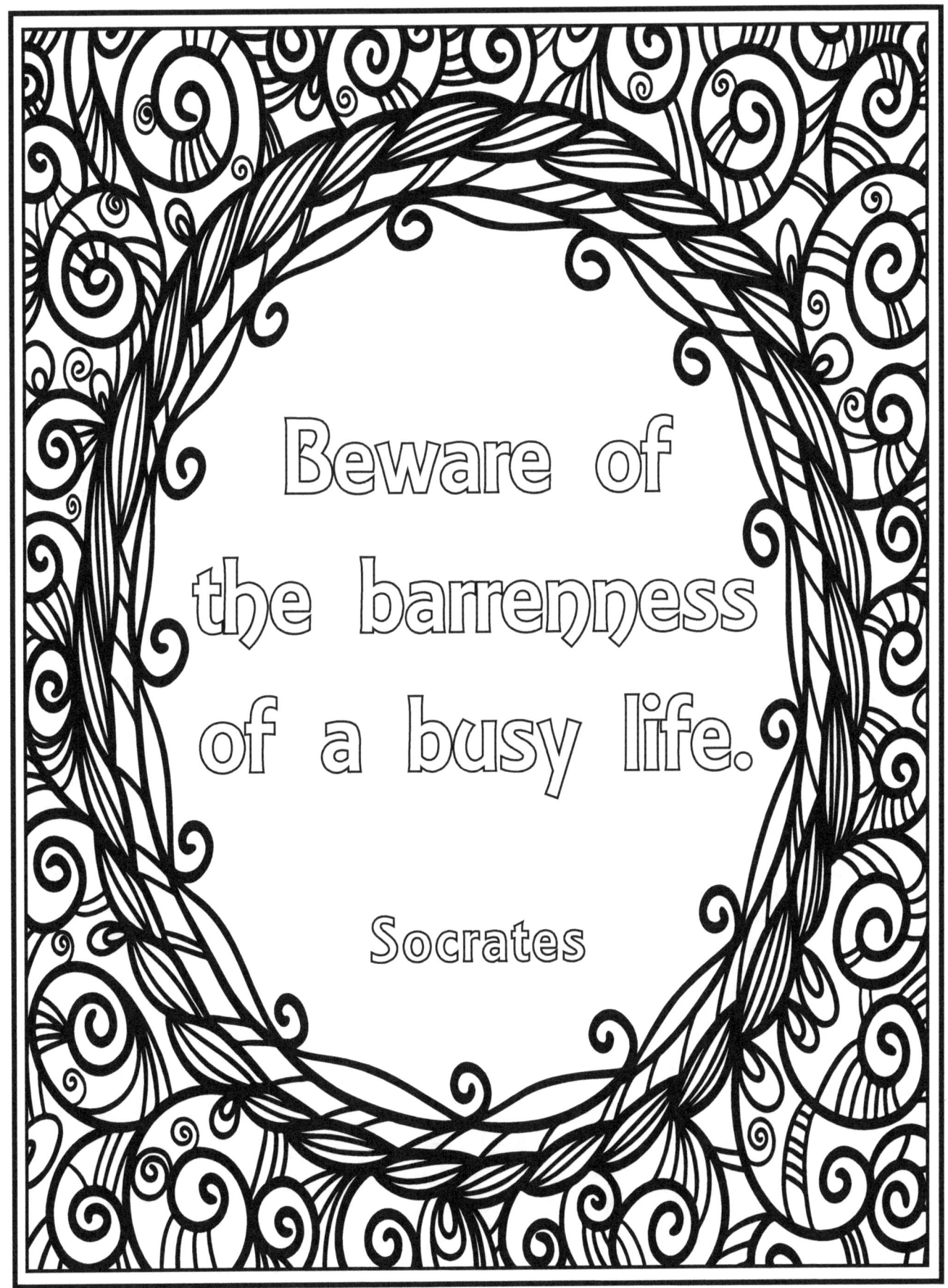

There are only two ways to live your life:

One is as though nothing is a miracle. The other is as though everything is a miracle.

Albert Einstein

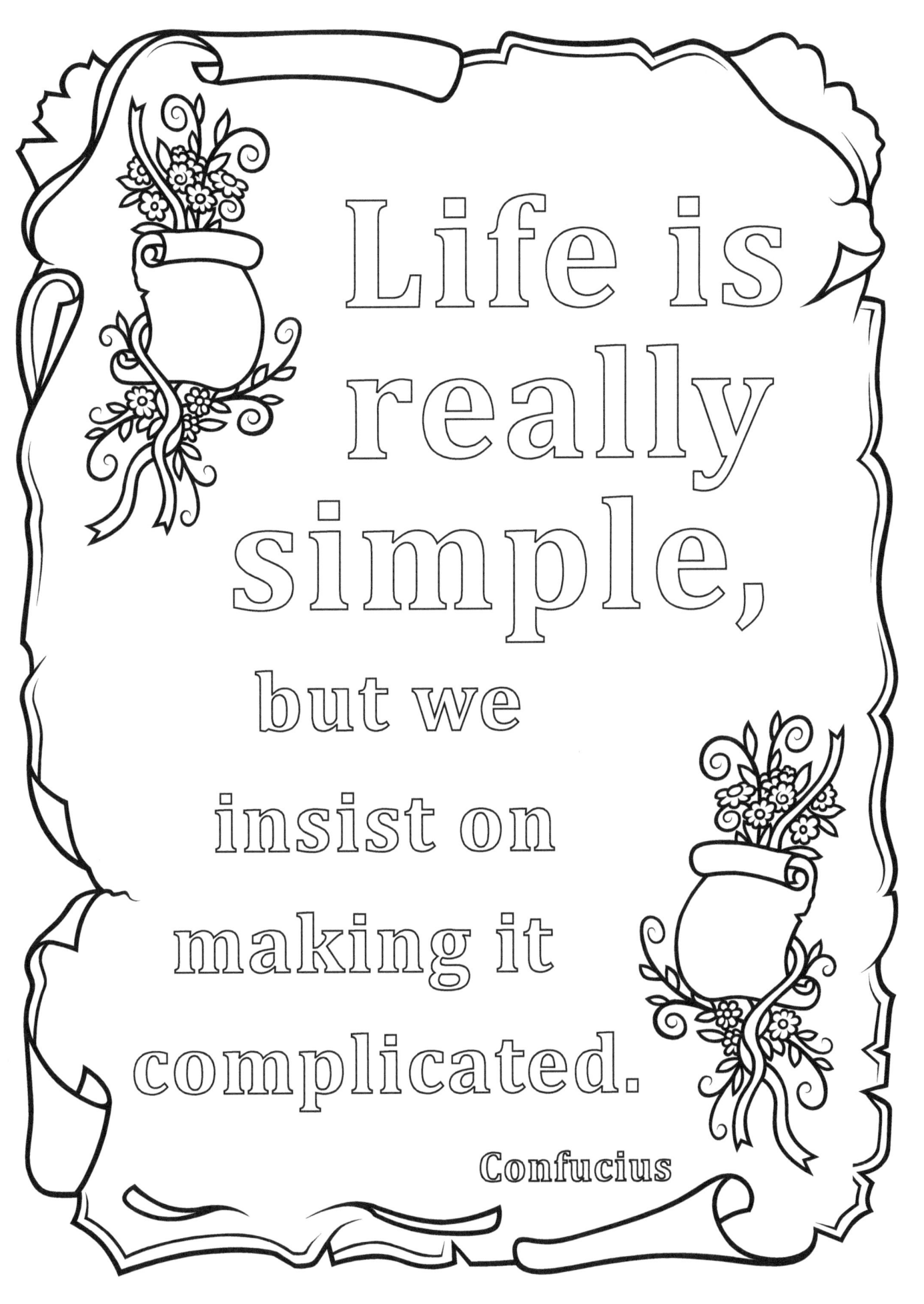

The only
journey is
the one within

Rainer Maria Rilke

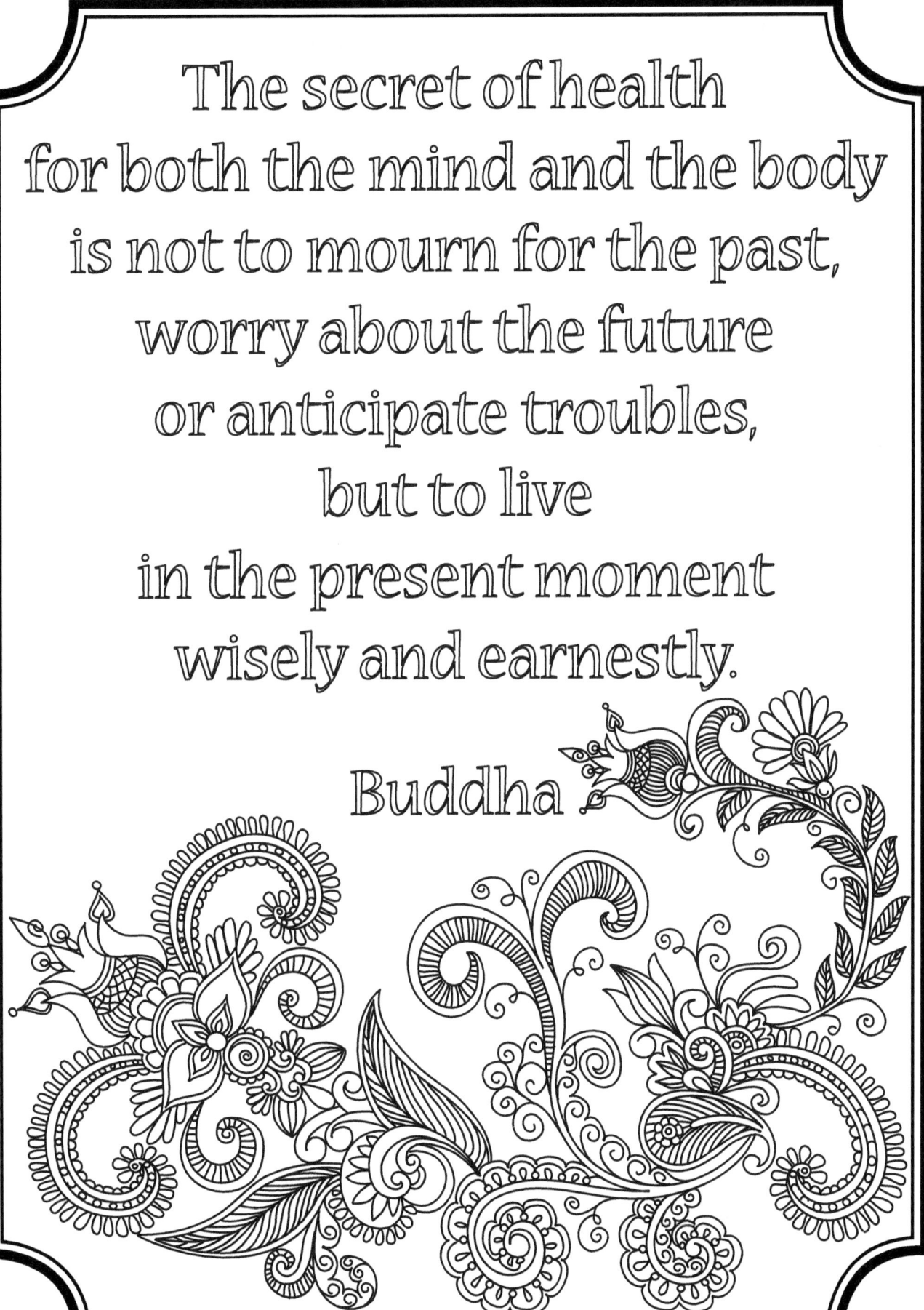

The secret of health
for both the mind and the body
is not to mourn for the past,
worry about the future
or anticipate troubles,
but to live
in the present moment
wisely and earnestly.

Buddha

Your breathing is your greatest friend. Return to it in all your troubles and you will find comfort and guidance.

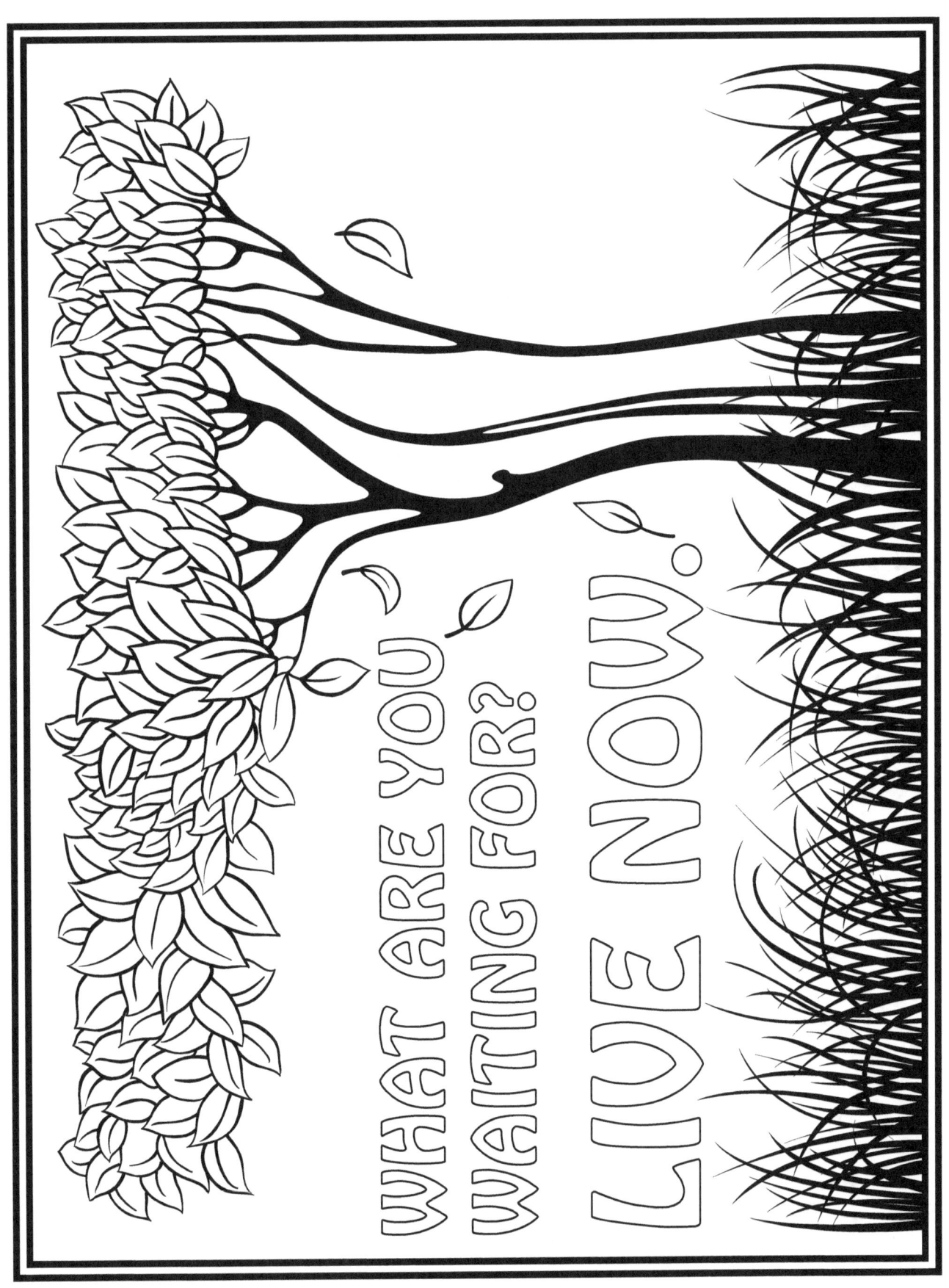

Every day is
a journey
and...

the journey itself
is home.

Matsuo Basho

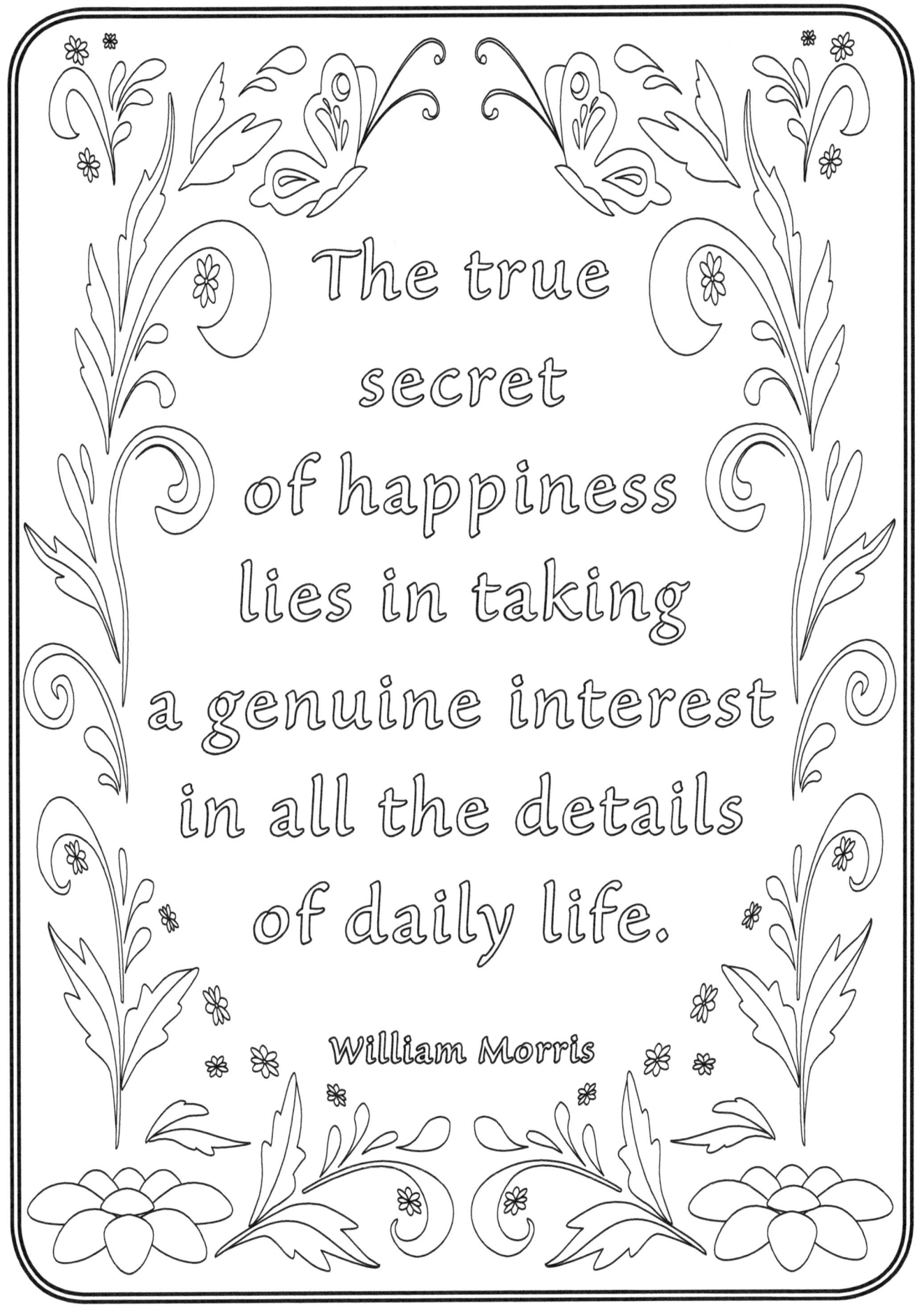

The true
secret
of happiness
lies in taking
a genuine interest
in all the details
of daily life.

William Morris

In the end,
it's not the years
in your life
that count.

IT'S THE LIFE
IN YOUR YEARS.

Abraham Lincoln

OUR GRAND BUSINESS IS NOT TO SEE WHAT LIES DIMLY AT A DISTANCE, BUT TO DO WHAT LIES CLEARLY AT HAND.

THOMAS CARLYLE

The meeting of two eternities, the past and future... is precisely the present moment.

Henry David Thoreau

LET REALITY BE REALITY.

LAO TZU

LET THINGS
FLOW NATURALLY FORWARD
IN WHATEVER WAY THEY LIKE.

Be happy for this moment.

THIS MOMENT IS YOUR LIFE.

Omar Khayyam

WHAT WE ARE TODAY
COMES FROM
OUR THOUGHTS OF YESTERDAY,
AND OUR PRESENT THOUGHTS
BUILD OUR LIFE OF TOMORROW.

OUR LIFE IS
THE CREATION
OF OUR MIND.

BUDDHA

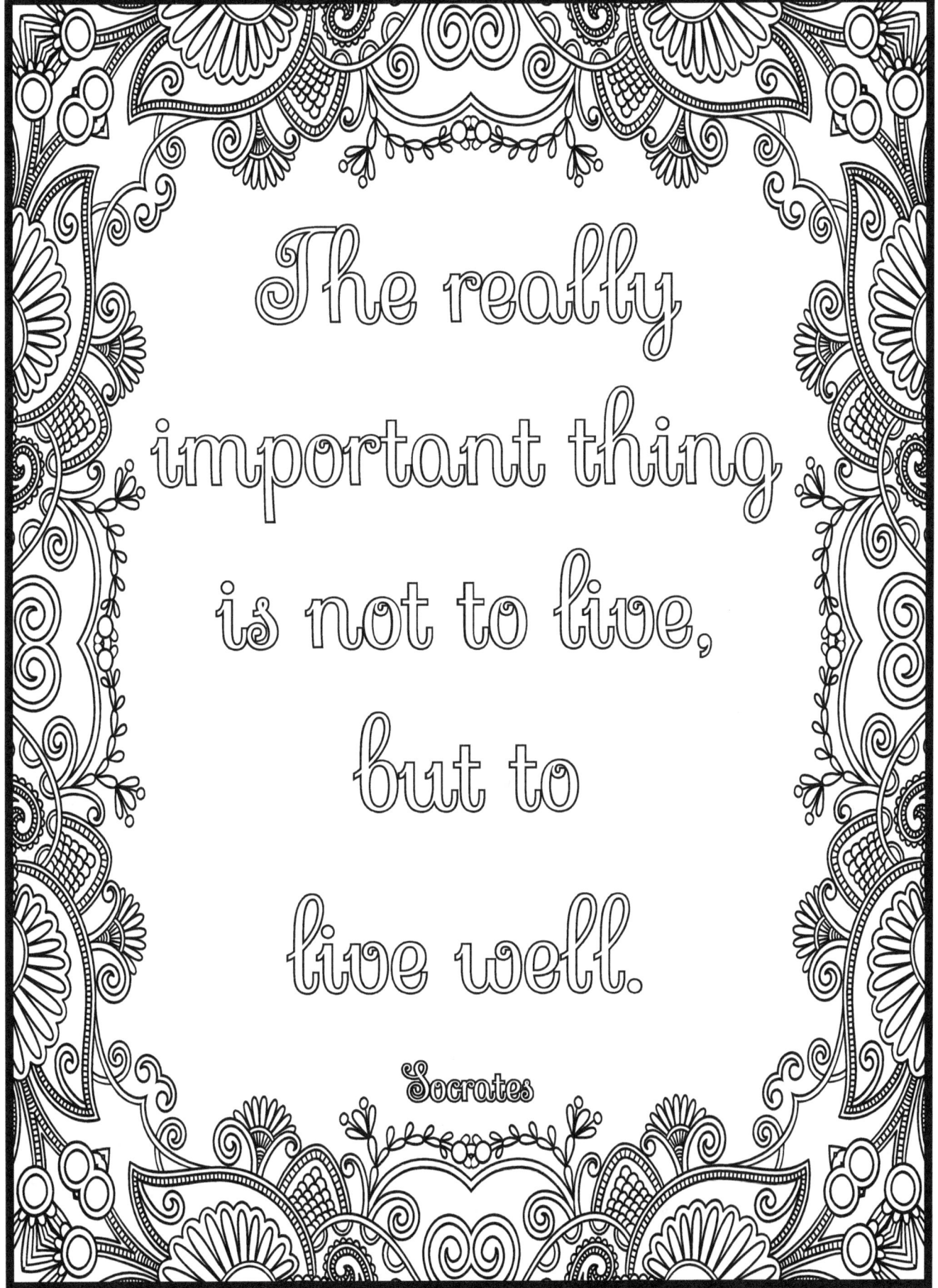

The really important thing is not to live, but to live well.

Socrates

Silence
is a true friend
who never betrays.

Confucius

THERE IS ONLY ONE TIME
THAT IS IMPORTANT —
NOW!

LEO
TOLSTOY

If you realize that
ALL THINGS CHANGE,
there is nothing
you will try to hold on to.

Lao Tzu

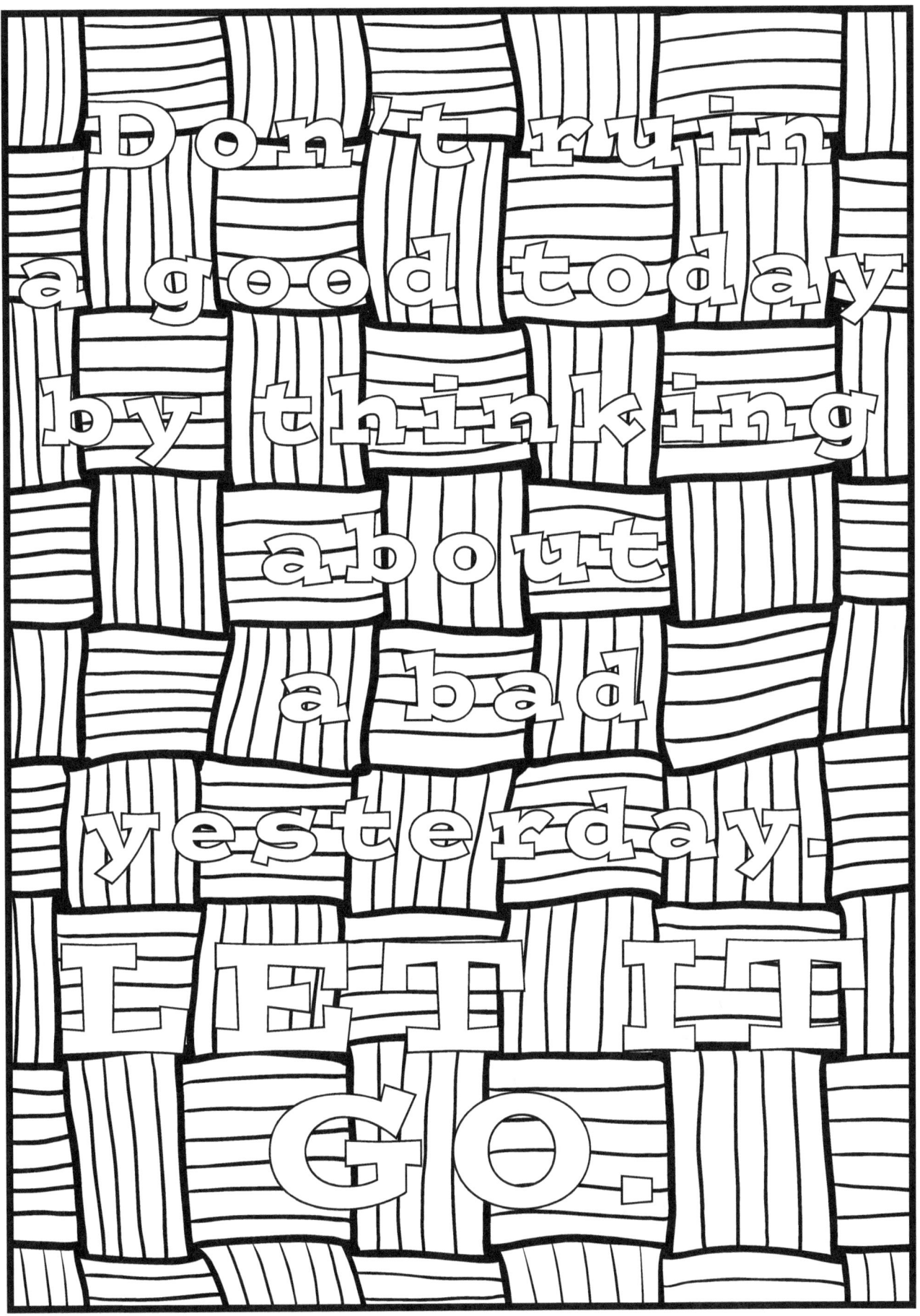

Sometimes the people around you won't understand your journey.

They don't need to;
it's not for them.

Take time to do what makes your soul happy.

We do not remember the day, we remember moments.

Cesare Pavese

Let life
happen to you.
Believe me: life is in the right,
always.

Rainer Maria Rilke

I WANT YOU TO BE
EVERYTHING
THAT'S YOU,

DEEP AT
THE CENTER OF
YOUR BEING.

CONFUCIUS

Visit Luscious Books' website

www.lusciousbooks.co.uk

for more colouring books and sample pages.